NO GALLBLADDER DIET

MAIN COURSE - Breakfast, Main Course, Dessert and Snacks Recipes for Gallbladder Disorders and surgery recovery

TABLE OF CONTENTS

BREAKFAST 6
MORNING MUFFINS 6
FIBER MUFFINS 8
RASPBERRY CRUMBLE 10
QUINOA CREPES WITH APPLESAUCE 12
MUFFINS WITH BANANAS 14
MORNING CARROT SALAD 16
MUESLI WITH RASPBERRIES 17
RASPBERRY MUFFINS 19
APPLE WITH CINNAMON 21
BUCKWHEAT PANCAKES WITH BANANAS 22
STRAWBERRY MUFFINS 24
CHOCOLATE MUFFINS 26
SIMPLE MUFFINS 28
SIMPLE OMELETTE 30
SPINACH OMELETTE 32
RED BELL PEPPER OMELETTE 34
CHEESE OMELETTE 36
CUCUMBER OMELETTE 38
CUCUMBER GUACAMOLE BITES 40
GREEK YOGURT AND TAHINI DIP 41
LUNCH 43
GREEN SOUP RECIPE 43
BEET RECIPE 44
MUSHROOM RISOTTO 45

ONION SOUP	47
SPICY SNOW PEAS	48
HONEY SAGE CARROTS	50
BLUEBERRY FRENCH TOAST	52
CHICKEN WITH WILD RICE	54
VEGETABLE KEBABS	56
BEEF AND VEGETABLE STEW	58
BROILED GROUPER	60
BROILED WHITE SEA BASS	61
BUCKWHEAT PANCAKES	62
BUTTERMILK WAFFLES	64
CHICKEN BRATS	66
CHICKEN STIR-FRY WITH EGGPLANT	68
CINNAMON FRENCH TOAST	70
COD WITH LEMON	72
MANGO TANGO SALAD	74
COUSCOUS SALAD	75
DINNER	77
CRAB SALAD	77
CUCUMBER PINEAPPLE SALAD	79
AVOCADO SALAD	80
SPINACH SALAD	81
CORN SALAD	82
BEET SALAD	83
RICE SALAD	84
CURRY CHICKEN SALAD	85

QUINOA SALAD	86
STRAWBERRY SALAD	87
SMOOTHIES	89
PUMPKIN PIE SMOOTHIE	89
LIVER CLENSE SMOOTHIE	90
CARROT SMOOTHIE	91
OATMEAL SMOOTHIE	92
ORANGE SMOOTHIE	93
BANANA SMOOTHIE	94
PEANUT BUTTER SMOOTHIE	95
BERRY SMOOTHIE	96
YOGURT SMOOTHIE	97
MORNING SMOOTHIE	98

☐ Copyright 2019 by Noah Jerris - All rights reserved.

This document is geared towards providing exact and reliable information in regards to the topic and issue covered. The publication is sold with the idea that the publisher is not required to render accounting, officially permitted, or otherwise, qualified services. If advice is necessary, legal or professional, a practiced individual in the profession should be ordered.

- From a Declaration of Principles which was accepted and approved equally by a Committee of the American Bar Association and a Committee of Publishers and Associations.

In no way is it legal to reproduce, duplicate, or transmit any part of this document in either electronic means or in printed format. Recording of this publication is strictly prohibited and any storage of this document is not allowed unless with written permission from the publisher. All rights reserved.

The information provided herein is stated to be truthful and consistent, in that any liability, in terms of inattention or otherwise, by any usage or abuse of any policies, processes, or directions contained within is the solitary and utter responsibility of the recipient reader. Under no circumstances will any legal responsibility or blame be held against the publisher for any reparation, damages, or monetary loss due to the information herein, either directly or indirectly.

Respective authors own all copyrights not held by the publisher.

The information herein is offered for informational purposes solely, and is universal as so. The presentation of the information is without contract or any type of guarantee assurance.

The trademarks that are used are without any consent, and the publication of the trademark is without permission or backing by the trademark owner. All trademarks and brands within this book are for clarifying purposes only and are the owned by the owners themselves, not affiliated with this document.

Introduction

No Gallbladder recipes for personal enjoyment but also for family enjoyment. You will love them for sure for how easy it is to prepare them.

BREAKFAST

MORNING MUFFINS

Serves: **8-12**

Prep Time: **10** Minutes

Cook Time: **25** Minutes

Total Time: **35** Minutes

INGREDIENTS

- 1 cup oats
- ¼ cup unsweetened applesauce
- 2 egg whites
- 1 cup oat milk
- 1 cup whole wheat flour
- ¼ cup brown sugar
- ¼ tsp baking soda
- ¼ tsp salt
- 1 tsp cinnamon
- ½ cup blueberries

DIRECTIONS

1. Preheat oven to 375 F
2. In a bowl combine all ingredients together and mix well
3. Fill 8-12 paper muffin cups with batter and fold in blueberries
4. Bake for 20-25 minutes
5. When ready remove and serve

FIBER MUFFINS

Serves: **8-12**

Prep Time: **5** Minutes

Cook Time: **15** Minutes

Total Time: **20** Minutes

INGREDIENTS

- 1 cup wheat bran
- 1cup nonfat milk
- ¼ cup unsweetened applesauce
- 1 egg
- ¼ cup brown sugar
- ¼ cup all-purpose flour
- ¼ cup whole wheat flour
- 1 tsp baking powder
- 1 tsp baking soda
- ¼ tsp salt
- 1 cup blueberries

DIRECTIONS

1. Preheat oven to 400 F
2. In a bowl combine wheat bran and milk and set aside
3. In another bowl combine egg, brown sugar, apple sauce and stir in bran mixture, mix well
4. In another bowl combine baking soda, baking powder, wheat flour, all-purpose flour and mix well
5. Stir flour mixture into bran and egg mixture and mix well
6. Fold in blueberries and fill muffin cups with batter
7. Bake for 12-15 minutes
8. When ready remove and serve

RASPBERRY CRUMBLE

Serves: **4**
Prep Time: **10**   Minutes
Cook Time: **50**   Minutes
Total Time: **60**   Minutes

INGREDIENTS

- 2 eggs
- 1 cup raspberries
- 1 cup apple juice
- 1 cup oats
- 1 tablespoon butter
- 1 tablespoon brown sugar
- 1 tablespoon cinnamon
- ¼ tsp cloves

DIRECTIONS

1. **Preheat oven to 375 F**
2. **In a bowl combine raspberries, apple slices and apple juice**

3. In another bowl combine sugar, spices, oats, butter and mix well
4. Cover apple slices with crumble topping
5. Bake for 45-50 minutes
6. When ready remove and serve

QUINOA CREPES WITH APPLESAUCE

Serves: **4**

Prep Time: **10** Minutes

Cook Time: **30** Minutes

Total Time: **40** Minutes

INGREDIENTS

- 1 cup quinoa flour
- ½ cup tapioca flour
- 1 tsp baking soda
- 1 tsp cinnamon
- 1 cup water
- 2 tablespoons canola oil
- 2 cups organic apple sauce

DIRECTIONS

1. In a bowl combine quinoa flour, baking soda, cinnamon, tapioca flour, water, oil and whisk well
2. Preheat a skillet over medium heat and pour ¼ cup batter into skillet

3. Cook each crepe on low heat for 1-2 minutes per side
4. When ready remove and serve with apple sauce

MUFFINS WITH BANANAS

Serves: **8-12**
Prep Time: **10** Minutes
Cook Time: **30** Minutes
Total Time: **40** Minutes

INGREDIENTS

- 1 cup whole wheat flour
- ¼ cup brown sugar
- ¼ tsp baking powder
- ¼ cup walnuts
- ¼ tsp salt
- 1 banana
- ¼ cup almond milk
- 1 egg
-

DIRECTIONS

1. Preheat oven to 375 F
2. In a bowl combine walnut, salt, flour, sugar, baking powder

3. In another bowl combine banana, eggs, almond milk and mix well
4. Combine dry and wet ingredients and mix well
5. Pour batter into a muffin pan and bake for 25-30 minutes or until golden brown
6. When ready remove and serve

MORNING CARROT SALAD

Serves: **2**

Prep Time: **5** Minutes

Cook Time: **5** Minutes

Total Time: **10** Minutes

INGREDIENTS

- 2 cups apples
- 2 cups carrot
- ¼ cup goji berries
- 4 tablespoons apple juice
- 1 tsp ginger
- 2 tablespoons olive oil

DIRECTIONS

1. **In a bowl combine all ingredients together**
2. **Mix well and add apple juice and olive oil**
3. **Serve when ready**

MUESLI WITH RASPBERRIES

Serves: **2-4**
Prep Time: **5** Minutes
Cook Time: **15** Minutes
Total Time: **20** Minutes

INGREDIENTS

- 1 cup oats
- ½ cup rice
- 1 tsp cinnamon
- 1 cup apples
- 1 cup cherries
- 1 cup raspberries
- 2 tablespoons brown sugar
- ¼ cup almond milk

DIRECTIONS

1. **Preheat oven to 300 F**
2. **In a bowl combine cinnamon, sugar and oats**
3. **Spread mixture onto a baking tray**

4. Toast oats for 8-10 minutes
5. When ready remove and set aside
6. Pour mixture into a bowl, top with apples, cherries, raspberries and serve with almond milk

RASPBERRY MUFFINS

Serves: *6-8*
Prep Time: *10*   Minutes
Cook Time: *15*   Minutes
Total Time: *25*   Minutes

INGREDIENTS

- 1 cup whole wheat flour
- ½ cup soy flour
- 1 tsp baking powder
- ½ cup brown sugar
- 1 tsp cinnamon
- 3 egg whites
- 1 cup soy milk
- 1 tablespoon canola oil
- 1 cup raspberries

DIRECTIONS

1. Preheat the oven to 400 F
2. In a bowl combine all dry ingredients

3. In another bowl combine all wet ingredients and mix with dry ingredients
4. Fold in raspberries and fill 8-12 muffin cups with batter
5. Bake for 12-15 minutes or until golden brown
6. When ready remove and serve

APPLE WITH CINNAMON

Serves: **4**
Prep Time: **10** Minutes
Cook Time: **30** Minutes
Total Time: **40** Minutes

INGREDIENTS

- 1 apple
- ¼ tsp cinnamon
- Pinch of brown sugar

DIRECTIONS

1. Place apple slices on a plate
2. Sprinkle with cinnamon and brown sugar
3. Serve when ready

BUCKWHEAT PANCAKES WITH BANANAS

Serves: **6**

Prep Time: **5** Minutes

Cook Time: **10** Minutes

Total Time: **15** Minutes

INGREDIENTS

- 1 cup buckwheat flour
- 1 tablespoon brown sugar
- ¼ tsp salt
- 1 tsp baking powder
- 1 cup almond milk
- 1 tablespoon canola oil
- 2 bananas

DIRECTIONS

1. In a bowl combine dry ingredients
2. Add wet ingredients and mix well
3. In a skillet pour ¼ cup batter and cook for 1-2 minutes per side

4. When ready remove and serve with syrup

STRAWBERRY MUFFINS

Serves: **8-12**

Prep Time: **10** Minutes

Cook Time: **20** Minutes

Total Time: **30** Minutes

INGREDIENTS

- 2 eggs
- 1 tablespoon olive oil
- 1 cup milk
- 2 cups whole wheat flour
- 1 tsp baking soda
- ¼ tsp baking soda
- 1 tsp cinnamon
- 1 cup strawberries

DIRECTIONS

1. In a bowl combine all dry ingredients
2. In another bowl combine all dry ingredients
3. Combine wet and dry ingredients together

4. Fold in strawberries and mix well
5. Pour mixture into 8-12 prepared muffin cups, fill 2/3 of the cups
6. Bake for 18-20 minutes at 375 F
7. When ready remove from the oven and serve

CHOCOLATE MUFFINS

Serves: **8-12**
Prep Time: **10** Minutes
Cook Time: **20** Minutes
Total Time: **30** Minutes

INGREDIENTS

- 2 eggs
- 1 tablespoon olive oil
- 1 cup milk
- 2 cups whole wheat flour
- 1 tsp baking soda
- ¼ tsp baking soda
- 1 tsp cinnamon
- 1 cup chocolate chips

DIRECTIONS

1. In a bowl combine all dry ingredients
2. In another bowl combine all dry ingredients
3. Combine wet and dry ingredients together

4. Fold in chocolate chips and mix well
5. Pour mixture into 8-12 prepared muffin cups, fill 2/3 of the cups
6. Bake for 18-20 minutes at 375 F
7. When ready remove from the oven and serve

SIMPLE MUFFINS

Serves: **8-12**
Prep Time: **10** Minutes
Cook Time: **20** Minutes
Total Time: **30** Minutes

INGREDIENTS

- 2 eggs
- 1 tablespoon olive oil
- 1 cup milk
- 2 cups whole wheat flour
- 1 tsp baking soda
- ¼ tsp baking soda
- 1 tsp cinnamon

DIRECTIONS

1. In a bowl combine all dry ingredients
2. In another bowl combine all dry ingredients
3. Combine wet and dry ingredients together

4. Pour mixture into 8-12 prepared muffin cups, fill 2/3 of the cups
5. Bake for 18-20 minutes at 375 F
6. When ready remove from the oven and serve

SIMPLE OMELETTE

Serves: **1**

Prep Time: **5** Minutes

Cook Time: **10** Minutes

Total Time: **15** Minutes

INGREDIENTS

- 2 eggs
- ¼ tsp salt
- ¼ tsp black pepper
- 1 tablespoon olive oil
- ¼ cup cheese
- ¼ tsp basil

DIRECTIONS

1. In a bowl combine all ingredients together and mix well
2. In a skillet heat olive oil and pour the egg mixture
3. Cook for 1-2 minutes per side

4. When ready remove omelette from the skillet and serve

SPINACH OMELETTE

Serves: **1**

Prep Time: **5** Minutes

Cook Time: **10** Minutes

Total Time: **15** Minutes

INGREDIENTS

- 2 eggs
- ¼ tsp salt
- ¼ tsp black pepper
- 1 tablespoon olive oil
- ¼ cup cheese
- ¼ tsp basil
- 1 cup spinach

DIRECTIONS

1. In a bowl combine all ingredients together and mix well
2. In a skillet heat olive oil and pour the egg mixture
3. Cook for 1-2 minutes per side

4. When ready remove omelette from the skillet and serve

RED BELL PEPPER OMELETTE

Serves: *1*

Prep Time: *5* Minutes

Cook Time: *10* Minutes

Total Time: *15* Minutes

INGREDIENTS

- 2 eggs
- ¼ tsp salt
- ¼ tsp black pepper
- 1 tablespoon olive oil
- ¼ cup cheese
- ¼ tsp basil
- 1 cup red bell pepper

DIRECTIONS

1. In a bowl combine all ingredients together and mix well
2. In a skillet heat olive oil and pour the egg mixture
3. Cook for 1-2 minutes per side

4. When ready remove omelette from the skillet and serve

CHEESE OMELETTE

Serves: **1**

Prep Time: **5** Minutes

Cook Time: **10** Minutes

Total Time: **15** Minutes

INGREDIENTS

- 2 eggs
- ¼ tsp salt
- ¼ tsp black pepper
- 1 tablespoon olive oil
- ¼ cup cheese
- ¼ tsp basil
- 1 cup low-fat cheese

DIRECTIONS

1. In a bowl combine all ingredients together and mix well
2. In a skillet heat olive oil and pour the egg mixture
3. Cook for 1-2 minutes per side

4. When ready remove omelette from the skillet and serve

CUCUMBER OMELETTE

Serves: **1**

Prep Time: **5** Minutes

Cook Time: **10** Minutes

Total Time: **15** Minutes

INGREDIENTS

- 2 eggs
- ¼ tsp salt
- ¼ tsp black pepper
- 1 tablespoon olive oil
- ¼ cup cheese
- ¼ tsp basil
- 1 cup cucumber

DIRECTIONS

1. In a bowl combine all ingredients together and mix well
2. In a skillet heat olive oil and pour the egg mixture
3. Cook for 1-2 minutes per side

4. When ready remove omelette from the skillet and serve

CUCUMBER GUACAMOLE BITES

Serves: **4-6**

Prep Time: **5** Minutes

Cook Time: **10** Minutes

Total Time: **15** Minutes

INGREDIENTS

- 1 cucumber
- 1 cup Cilantro
- Chile powder

DIRECTIONS

1. Slice the cucumber into thick slices
2. Scoop out the center of the cucumber slice
3. Fill each cucumber slice with guacamole
4. Sprinkle with chile powder and serve

GREEK YOGURT AND TAHINI DIP

Serves: *1*
Prep Time: *5* Minutes
Cook Time: *5* Minutes
Total Time: *10* Minutes

INGREDIENTS

- 1 cup Greek Yogurt
- ¼ cup green onion
- ¼ cup sour cream
- 1 tablespoon olive oil
- 1 tablespoon tahini paste
- 2-3 tomatoes
- 1 large cucumber

DIRECTIONS

1. In a bowl whisk together tahini paste, sour cream, olive oil and mix well
2. Add Greek yogurt, green onion and mix well
3. Serve with tomatoes or cucumbers

LUNCH

GREEN SOUP RECIPE

Serves: 2
Prep Time: 5 Minutes
Cook Time: 10 Minutes
Total Time: 15 Minutes

INGREDIENTS

- One bunch parsley
- 2 zucchini
- ¼ lb. green beans
- 4 stalks celery

DIRECTIONS

1. Steam all ingredients for 10 minutes
2. When ready, pure in a blender
3. Add 2-3 drops of lemon juice and serve

BEET RECIPE

Serves: **2**

Prep Time: **5** Minutes

Cook Time: **5** Minutes

Total Time: **10** Minutes

INGREDIENTS

- 2 lbs. raw beet
- Lemon juice
- Flax oil

DIRECTIONS

1. Using a blender puree your beets
2. Add lemon juice and flax oil, mix well
3. When ready serve with salad

MUSHROOM RISOTTO

Serves: **2**
Prep Time: **10** Minutes
Cook Time: **20** Minutes
Total Time: **30** Minutes

INGREDIENTS

- 2 tablespoons olive oil
- 2 lb. crimini mushrooms
- 1 garlic clove
- 1 cup brown rice
- 4 cups vegetable broth
- 2 tablespoons parsley
- ½ lb. frozen peas
- Salt

DIRECTIONS

1. In a saucepan add mushrooms, salt, pepper and cook until mushrooms are soft
2. Transfer to a place

3. In a same saucepan heat olive oil, onion, garlic and sauté for 2-3 minutes, add rice, broth and cook until broth is absorbed
4. Add peas, mushrooms and cook for a couples of minutes
5. Transfer to a place, garnish with parsley and serve

ONION SOUP

Serves: **6**

Prep Time: **10** Minutes

Cook Time: **20** Minutes

Total Time: **30** Minutes

INGREDIENTS

- 1 tablespoon canola oil
- 2 onions
- 1 leek
- ¼ tablespoons rosemary
- ¼ tablespoon thyme
- 2 apples
- 5 cups vegetable broth

DIRECTIONS

1. In a saucepan sauté onion, pour broth and bring to boil
2. Add apples and the rest of ingredients and simmer on low heat for 15-20 minutes
3. When ready remove from heat and serve

SPICY SNOW PEAS

Serves: **5**

Prep Time: **10** Minutes

Cook Time: **20** Minutes

Total Time: **30** Minutes

INGREDIENTS

- 1 lb. snow peas
- 2 tablespoons soy sauce
- 2 tablespoons rice vinegar
- 2 tablespoons brown sugar
- 1 tablespoon cornstarch
- 1 tsp sesame oil
- 1 garlic clove

DIRECTIONS

1. In a saucepan bring water to a boil, add peas, reduce heat and simmer for 4-5 minutes
2. In another bowl combine rice vinegar, soy sauce, cornstarch, sugar, spices and mix well
3. In a skillet heat sesame oil, add garlic and peas

4. Pour in the soy sauce mixture and cook for 4-5 minutes
5. Remove from wheat and serve

HONEY SAGE CARROTS

Serves: **5**
Prep Time: **10** Minutes
Cook Time: **20** Minutes
Total Time: **30** Minutes

INGREDIENTS

- 2 cups carrots
- 2 tsp butter
- 2 tablespoons honey
- 1 tablespoon sage
- ½ tsp black pepper
- ¼ tsp salt

DIRECTIONS

1. In a pot bring water to a boil
2. Add carrots and sauté for 5-6 minutes
3. In a pan transfer the carrots in melted butter
4. Add honey, sage, pepper and cook for 4-5 minutes

5. When ready remove from heat and serve

BLUEBERRY FRENCH TOAST

Serves: **4**

Prep Time: **10** Minutes

Cook Time: **25** Minutes

Total Time: **35** Minutes

INGREDIENTS

- French baguette
- 2 egg whites
- 1 cup soy milk
- ½ tsp nutmeg
- 1 tsp vanilla
- 2 tablespoons brown sugar
- ½ cup blueberries
- 1 tablespoon canola oil
- ½ cup pecans

DIRECTIONS

1. In a bowl whisk egg whites with milk, vanilla, brown sugar and nutmeg

2. Pour mixture over bread and let it chill overnight
3. Fold in blueberries and spoon pecans into bread
4. Bake at 375 F for 20-25 minutes
5. When ready remove and serve

CHICKEN WITH WILD RICE

Serves: **4**
Prep Time: **10** Minutes
Cook Time: **90** Minutes
Total Time: **10** Minutes

INGREDIENTS

- 1 lb. chicken breast
- 1 cup celery
- 1 cup onions
- 1 tsp tarragon
- 1 cup chicken broth
- 1 cup white wine
- ½ cup long grain rice
- ½ cup wild rice

DIRECTIONS

1. Preheat oven to 325 F
2. In a bowl combine celery, onions, tarragon, chicken, chicken broth and pour mixture in a frying pan

3. Cook for 10-12 minutes
4. In a baking dish combine 1 cup chicken broth, rice, wine and soak for 20-30 minutes
5. Add cooked chicken and bake for 50-60 minutes
6. When ready remove and serve

VEGETABLE KEBABS

Serves: **2**

Prep Time: **10** Minutes

Cook Time: **80** Minutes

Total Time: **90** Minutes

INGREDIENTS

- 2 cups water
- ¼ cup brown rice
- 5 oz. top sirloin
- 2 tablespoons Italian dressing
- 1 green pepper
- 2 tomatoes
- 1 onion
- 2 wooden skewers

DIRECTIONS

1. In a saucepan bring water to a boil and add rice
2. Reduce heat and simmer for 35-40 minutes
3. Transfer to a bowl and set aside

4. Cut the meat and pour Italian dressing and refrigerate for 20-30 minutes
5. Thread 2 cubes of meat 2 tomato halves, 2 onion, 2 green pepper pieces onto each skewer and grill for 5-10 minutes
6. When ready remove from heat and serve

BEEF AND VEGETABLE STEW

Serves: **6**

Prep Time: **10** Minutes

Cook Time: **50** Minutes

Total Time: **60** Minutes

INGREDIENTS

- 1 lb. beef
- 1 tsp canola oil
- 2 cups onion
- 1 cup celery
- 1 cup tomatoes
- ¼ cup sweet potato
- ¼ cup mushrooms
- 1 cup carrot
- 2 cloves garlic
- 1 cup kale
- ¼ cup red wine vinegar
- 1 tsp balsamic vinegar
- 2 cups low-sodium vegetable stock
- 1 tsp thyme

- 1 tsp parsley
- 1 tsp oregano
- 1 tsp rosemary

DIRECTIONS

1. In a pot, sauté vegetables over medium heat for 10-12 minutes
2. Cut steak into pieces and add to pot
3. Add vinegar, herbs, stock, spices and bring to a boil
4. Simmer for 40-50 minutes
5. When ready remove from heat and serve

BROILED GROUPER

Serves: **4**

Prep Time: **10** Minutes

Cook Time: **40** Minutes

Total Time: **50** Minutes

INGREDIENTS

- 2 lemon wedges
- 1 tablespoon low-sodium teriyaki sauce
- ¼ tsp garlic
- 2 grouper fillets
- ½ tsp Italian seasoning

DIRECTIONS

1. In a bowl combine garlic and teriyaki sauce
2. Place grouper fillets in the pan and brush with teriyaki marinade both sides
3. Cover and refrigerate for 20-30 minutes
4. Grill for 10 minutes per side
5. When ready remove from heat and serve with Italian seasoning

BROILED WHITE SEA BASS

Serves: **2**

Prep Time: **10** Minutes

Cook Time: **15** Minutes

Total Time: **25** Minutes

INGREDIENTS

- 2 white sea bass fillets
- 1 tablespoon lemon juice
- 1 tsp garlic
- ½ tsp herb seasoning
- black pepper

DIRECTIONS

1. Place the fillets in the pan
2. Sprinkle with garlic, lemon juice, seasoning and grill for 10 minutes per side
3. When ready remove from heat and serve

BUCKWHEAT PANCAKES

Serves: **4**

Prep Time: **10** Minutes

Cook Time: **20** Minutes

Total Time: **30** Minutes

INGREDIENTS

- 2 egg whites
- 1 tablespoon canola oil
- ¼ cup almond milk
- ¼ cup all-purpose flour
- ¼ cup buckwheat flour
- 1 tablespoon baking powder
- 1 tablespoon sugar
- ¼ cup water
- 2 cups strawberries

DIRECTIONS

1. In a bowl combine milk, egg whites, canola oil and mix well

2. In another bowl combine flours, sugar, baking powder, add egg white mixture, water and mix well
3. Pour ¼ cup pancake batter into a pan over low heat
4. Cook for 2-3 minutes per side
5. When ready remove and serve with strawberries

BUTTERMILK WAFFLES

Serves: **6**

Prep Time: **10** Minutes

Cook Time: **20** Minutes

Total Time: **30** Minutes

INGREDIENTS

- 1 cup whole-wheat flour
- 1 cup all-purpose flour
- 1 tsp baking powder
- ¼ tsp baking soda
- 1 tablespoon sugar
- 1 cup buttermilk
- 1 egg
- 4-6 egg whites

DIRECTIONS

1. In a bowl combine baking powder, baking soda, sugar, flours and mix well
2. In another bowl combine the egg, buttermilk and flour mixture, stir to mix evenly

3. In a bowl beat egg whites until stiff peaks form, fold the egg whites into the flour mixture
4. Preheat a waffle iron to 250 F
5. Spoon about ¾ cup of the batter into the waffle iron and cook according to the instructions
6. When ready remove and serve

CHICKEN BRATS

Serves: **6**

Prep Time: **10** Minutes

Cook Time: **15** Minutes

Total Time: **25** Minutes

INGREDIENTS

- 1 cup onion
- 2 cloves garlic
- ¼ tsp canola oil
- 1 cup cooked rice
- 1 lb. chicken breast
- 1 tsp cumin seed
- 1 tsp ground paprika
- 1 tsp black pepper
- ¼ tsp cayenne pepper
- 1 tsp rosemary
- ½ tsp nutmeg
- 1 tsp mustard
- 1 tsp celery seed

DIRECTIONS

1. In a pan sauté garlic and onion in canola oil
2. Transfer to a bowl and mix with rice, chicken breast and remaining ingredients
3. Refrigerate for 1-2 hours
4. Divide mixture into 6 portions and form 6 sausage shapes
5. Roast in oven at 325 F for 10-12 minutes
6. Transfer to a grill and cook for a couple of more minutes
7. When ready remove from heat and serve

CHICKEN STIR-FRY WITH EGGPLANT

Serves: **4**

Prep Time: **10** Minutes

Cook Time: **15** Minutes

Total Time: **25** Minutes

INGREDIENTS

- ½ cup basil
- 2 tablespoons mint
- ½ cup low-sodium vegetable stock
- 2 green onions
- 3 cloves garlic
- 1 tablespoon chopped ginger
- 1 tablespoon olive oil
- 1 eggplant
- 1 red bell pepper
- 1 lb. chicken breast
- 1 tablespoon soy sauce

DIRECTIONS

1. In a blender combine mint, stock, green onions, basil, garlic and ginger, blend until smooth
2. In a pan heat olive oil, add onion, bell peppers, eggplant and sauté until tender
3. Add basil mixture and sauté for 2-3 minutes
4. Add chicken strips, soy sauce and cook for another 2-3 minutes
5. Add remaining stock and bring to a boil
6. When ready transfer to a serving dish and garnish with green onion

CINNAMON FRENCH TOAST

Serves: **4**

Prep Time: **5** Minutes

Cook Time: **15** Minutes

Total Time: **20** Minutes

INGREDIENTS

- 4 egg whites
- 1 tsp vanilla
- ¼ tsp nutmeg
- 4 slices bread
- ½ tsp cinnamon
- ¼ cup maple syrup

DIRECTIONS

1. In a bowl combine vanilla, nutmeg, egg whites and whisk well
2. Dip the bread into the egg mixture
3. In a frying pan add the bread and sprinkle with cinnamon
4. Cook for 4-5 minutes per side

5. When ready remove and serve with maple syrup

COD WITH LEMON

Serves: **2**

Prep Time: **10** Minutes

Cook Time: **30** Minutes

Total Time: **40** Minutes

INGREDIENTS

- 2 lemons
- 2 cod fillets
- 1 tsp low-sodium bouillon granules
- 1 cup water
- 1 tablespoon butter
- 1 tablespoon all-purpose flour
- 2 tsp capers

DIRECTIONS

1. **Preheat the oven to 325 F**
2. **Squeeze juice from one lemon over cod fillet**
3. **Place fish in the oven and bake for 20-22 minutes**

4. While fish is cooking in a bowl combine chicken bouillon granules and water, set aside
5. In another bowl combine flour and butter
6. Transfer to a saucepan, add capers and bouillon to the butter mixture and continue to stir
7. When ready remove from heat and serve with the fish

MANGO TANGO SALAD

Serves: **4**

Prep Time: **10** Minutes

Cook Time: **30** Minutes

Total Time: **40** Minutes

INGREDIENTS

- 2 mangoes
- Juice of 1 lemon
- ¼ onion
- 1 tablespoon cilantro laves

DIRECTIONS

1. In a bowl combine all salad ingredients and mix well
2. Add salad dressing and serve when ready

COUSCOUS SALAD

Serves: **4**
Prep Time: **10** Minutes
Cook Time: **30** Minutes
Total Time: **40** Minutes

INGREDIENTS

- 1 cup couscous
- 1 cup zucchini
- 1 red bell pepper
- ¼ cup red onion
- ¼ tsp cumin
- ¼ tsp black pepper
- ¼ cup salad dressing
- ¼ tsp parsley

DIRECTIONS

1. In a bowl combine all salad ingredients and mix well
2. Add salad dressing and serve when ready

DINNER

CRAB SALAD

Serves: **2**
Prep Time: **10** Minutes
Cook Time: **30** Minutes
Total Time: **40** Minutes

INGREDIENTS

- ¼ cup lemon juice
- ¼ cup rice wine vinegar
- 1 tsp sugar
- 1 cucumber
- ¼ cup mint
- 10 oz. cooked crab
- 2 cups mixed salad greens
- 2 lime wedges

DIRECTIONS

1. In a bowl combine all salad ingredients and mix well

2. Add salad dressing and serve when ready

CUCUMBER PINEAPPLE SALAD

Serves: **4**

Prep Time: **10** Minutes

Cook Time: **30** Minutes

Total Time: **40** Minutes

INGREDIENTS

- ¼ cup sugar
- ¼ cup rice wine vinegar
- 1 cup pineapple
- 1 cucumber
- 1 carrot
- ¼ cup onion
- 2 cups salad greens
- 1 tablespoon sesame seeds

DIRECTIONS

1. In a bowl combine all salad ingredients and mix well
2. Add salad dressing and serve when ready

AVOCADO SALAD

Serves: **2**

Prep Time: **5** Minutes

Cook Time: **5** Minutes

Total Time: **10** Minutes

INGREDIENTS

- ½ avocado
- ½ onion
- 1 green bell pepper
- 2 tomatoes
- ¼ lime
- ¼ cup cilantro

DIRECTIONS

1. In a bowl combine all salad ingredients and mix well
2. Add salad dressing and serve when ready

SPINACH SALAD

Serves: *2*
Prep Time: *5* Minutes
Cook Time: *5* Minutes
Total Time: *10* Minutes

INGREDIENTS

- 1 peach
- ¼ cup pecans
- 2 cups spinach
- ¼ cup salad dressing
- ¼ cup tomatoes
- ¼ cup cucumber

DIRECTIONS

1. In a bowl combine all salad ingredients and mix well
2. Add salad dressing and serve when ready

CORN SALAD

Serves: **2**

Prep Time: **5** Minutes

Cook Time: **5** Minutes

Total Time: **10** Minutes

INGREDIENTS

- 5 ears corn
- 2 tomatoes
- ¼ onion
- ¼ cup basil
- ¼ cup olive oil
- ½ cup salad dressing

DIRECTIONS

1. **In a bowl combine all salad ingredients and mix well**
2. **Add salad dressing and serve when ready**

BEET SALAD

Serves: **2**

Prep Time: **5** Minutes

Cook Time: **5** Minutes

Total Time: **10** Minutes

INGREDIENTS

- 2 beets
- ¼ cup walnuts
- 2 tablespoons maple syrup
- 1 cup baby salad greens
- ¼ cup salad dressing
- ¼ cup low-fat cheese

DIRECTIONS

1. In a bowl combine all salad ingredients and mix well
2. Add salad dressing and serve when ready

RICE SALAD

Serves: **4**

Prep Time: **10** Minutes

Cook Time: **30** Minutes

Total Time: **40** Minutes

INGREDIENTS

- 1 cup wild rice
- ¼ cup white vinegar
- 1 tsp pepper
- 1 cup cooked chicken breast
- ¼ cup onion
- 1 cup almonds

DIRECTIONS

1. In a bowl combine all salad ingredients and mix well
2. Add salad dressing and serve when ready

CURRY CHICKEN SALAD

Serves: 2
Prep Time: 5 Minutes
Cook Time: 5 Minutes
Total Time: 10 Minutes

INGREDIENTS

- 2 chicken breasts
- 1 stalk celery
- 2 green onions
- ¼ cup raisins
- ¼ cup pecans
- ¼ tsp curry powder

DIRECTIONS

1. In a bowl combine all salad ingredients and mix well
2. Add salad dressing and serve when ready

QUINOA SALAD

Serves: **4**

Prep Time: **10** Minutes

Cook Time: **30** Minutes

Total Time: **40** Minutes

INGREDIENTS

- 1 cup cooked quinoa
- ¼ red bell pepper
- ¼ yellow bell pepper
- ¼ red onion
- ¼ cup cilantro
- ¼ lime juice
- ¼ cup cranberries

DIRECTIONS

1. In a bowl combine all salad ingredients and mix well
2. Add salad dressing and serve when ready

STRAWBERRY SALAD

Serves: **4**

Prep Time: **10** Minutes

Cook Time: **30** Minutes

Total Time: **40** Minutes

INGREDIENTS

- 1 tablespoon sesame seeds
- 1 tablespoon poppy seeds
- ¼ cup olive oil
- 8 oz. spinach
- 1 cup strawberries
- ½ cup almonds

DIRECTIONS

1. In a bowl combine all salad ingredients and mix well
2. Add salad dressing and serve when ready

SMOOTHIES

PUMPKIN PIE SMOOTHIE

Serves: *1*
Prep Time: *5* Minutes
Cook Time: *5* Minutes
Total Time: *10* Minutes

INGREDIENTS

- 1 can pumpkin
- 1 can evaporated fat free milk
- 1 cup non-fat yogurt
- ¼ tsp pumpkin pie spice
- 2 tablespoons whipped cream

DIRECTIONS

1. **In a blender place all ingredients and blend until smooth**
2. **Pour smoothie in a glass and serve**

LIVER CLENSE SMOOTHIE

Serves: *1*

Prep Time: *5* Minutes

Cook Time: *5* Minutes

Total Time: *10* Minutes

INGREDIENTS

- 4 cups water
- 2 lemons
- 1 cup parsley
- 4 celery stalks

DIRECTIONS

1. **In a blender place all ingredients and blend until smooth**
2. **Pour smoothie in a glass and serve**

CARROT SMOOTHIE

Serves: **1**
Prep Time: **5** Minutes
Cook Time: **5** Minutes
Total Time: **10** Minutes

INGREDIENTS

- 2 carrots
- 2 celery stalks
- 1 orange
- 1 lemon

DIRECTIONS

1. **In a blender place all ingredients and blend until smooth**
2. **Pour smoothie in a glass and serve**

OATMEAL SMOOTHIE

Serves: **1**

Prep Time: **5** Minutes

Cook Time: **5** Minutes

Total Time: **10** Minutes

INGREDIENTS

- 1 cup oatmeal
- ¼ cup Greek yogurt
- 1 cup milk
- 1 cup strawberries

DIRECTIONS

1. **In a blender place all ingredients and blend until smooth**
2. **Pour smoothie in a glass and serve**

ORANGE SMOOTHIE

Serves: **1**

Prep Time: **5** Minutes

Cook Time: **5** Minutes

Total Time: **10** Minutes

INGREDIENTS

- ½ cup orange juice
- 1 cup strawberries
- 1 cup ice
- 1 cup mango

DIRECTIONS

1. **In a blender place all ingredients and blend until smooth**
2. **Pour smoothie in a glass and serve**

BANANA SMOOTHIE

Serves: **1**

Prep Time: **5** Minutes

Cook Time: **5** Minutes

Total Time: **10** Minutes

INGREDIENTS

- 1 cup ice
- 1 cup skim milk
- 1 banana
- ½ tsp vanilla extract

DIRECTIONS

1. **In a blender place all ingredients and blend until smooth**
2. **Pour smoothie in a glass and serve**

PEANUT BUTTER SMOOTHIE

Serves: *1*

Prep Time: *5* Minutes

Cook Time: *5* Minutes

Total Time: *10* Minutes

INGREDIENTS

- 1 banana
- 1 cup milk
- 1 cup protein
- 1 tablespoon peanut butter

DIRECTIONS

1. **In a blender place all ingredients and blend until smooth**
2. **Pour smoothie in a glass and serve**

BERRY SMOOTHIE

Serves: **1**

Prep Time: **5** Minutes

Cook Time: **5** Minutes

Total Time: **10** Minutes

INGREDIENTS

- 2 cups orange juice
- 1 cup vanilla yogurt
- 1 banana
- 1 cup berries

DIRECTIONS

1. **In a blender place all ingredients and blend until smooth**
2. **Pour smoothie in a glass and serve**

YOGURT SMOOTHIE

Serves: **1**

Prep Time: **5** Minutes

Cook Time: **5** Minutes

Total Time: **10** Minutes

INGREDIENTS

- 1 banana
- 1 cup yogurt
- 1 cup almonds
- ½ cup milk
- ¼ cup raisins

DIRECTIONS

1. **In a blender place all ingredients and blend until smooth**
2. **Pour smoothie in a glass and serve**

MORNING SMOOTHIE

Serves: **1**

Prep Time: **5** Minutes

Cook Time: **5** Minutes

Total Time: **10** Minutes

INGREDIENTS

- 1 cup orange juice
- 1 cup berries
- 1 cup strawberry yogurt
- 1 tablespoon honey

DIRECTIONS

1. **In a blender place all ingredients and blend until smooth**
2. **Pour smoothie in a glass and serve**

THANK YOU FOR READING THIS BOOK!

Printed in Great Britain
by Amazon